LEGACY JOURNAL

Dr. Fatima A. McCoy-Leonard

Copyright © 2023 Dr. Fatima A. McCoy-Leonard

ALL RIGHTS RESERVED. This book contains material protected under International and Federal Copyright Laws and Treaties. Any unauthorized reprint or use of this material is prohibited. No part of this book may be reproduced or transmitted in any form or by any means, electronic or mechanical, including photocopying, recording, or by any information storage and retrieval system without express written permission from the author/publisher.

Scripture quotations are from the Holy Bible, New International Version®, NIV®. Copyright ©1973, 1978, 1984, 2011 by Biblica, Inc.™ Used by permission of Zondervan. All rights reserved worldwide. www.zondervan.com The "NIV" and "New International Version" are trademarks registered in the United States Patent and Trademark Office by Biblica, Inc.™

Book Cover Design: Prize Publishing House

Printed by: Prize Publishing House, LLC in the United States of America.

First printing edition 2023.

Prize Publishing House
P.O. Box 9856, Chesapeake, VA 23321
www.PrizePublishingHouse.com

ISBN (Hardcover): 979-8-9884324-2-5
ISBN (E-Book): 979-8-9884324-3-2

With God, all things are possible.
—Matthew 19:26

Arise, be of good courage, and do it.
—Ezra 10:4

My dreams are attainable.
I need to stay committed
to achieving them.

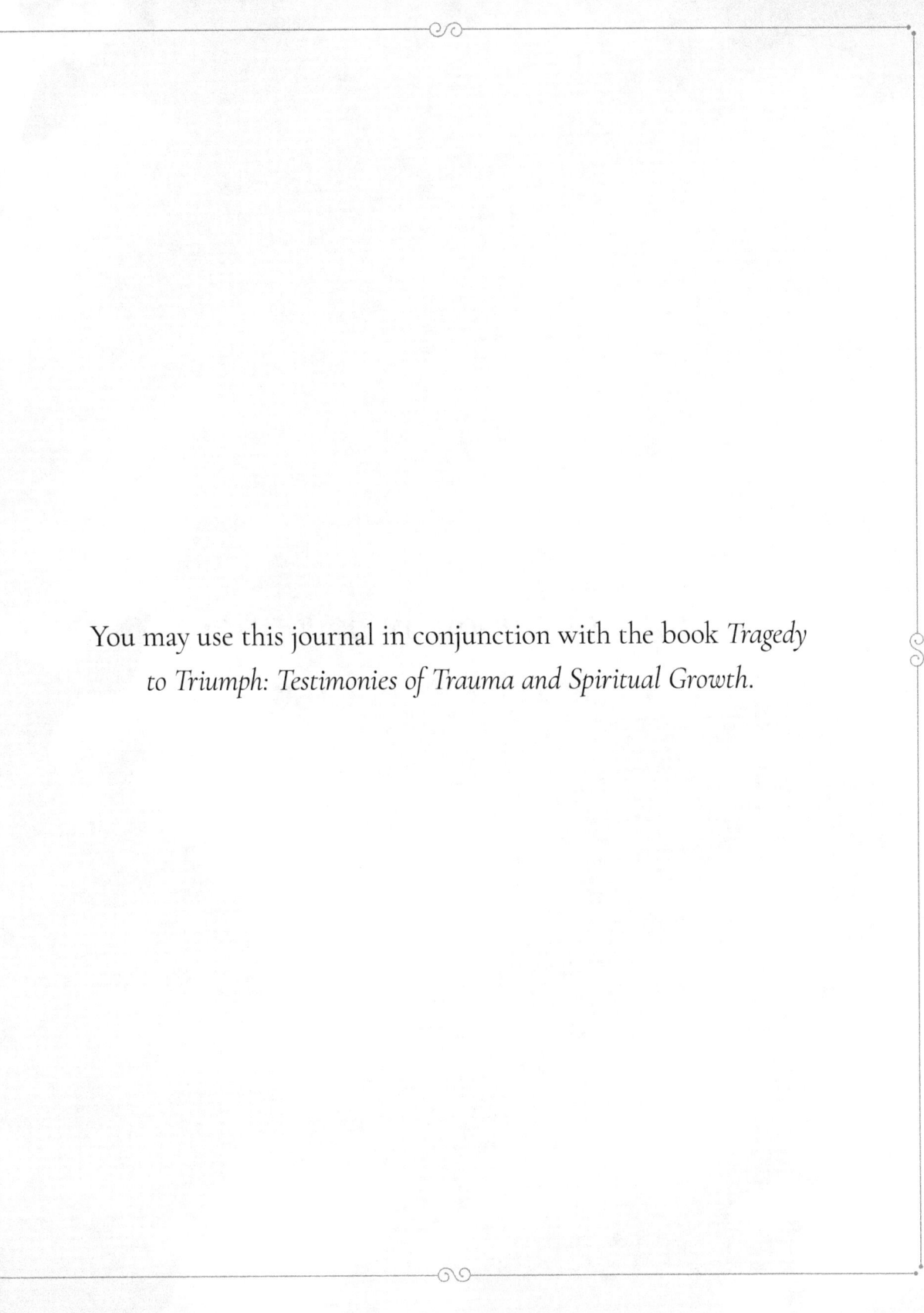

You may use this journal in conjunction with the book *Tragedy to Triumph: Testimonies of Trauma and Spiritual Growth.*

I am continuously becoming
a better me. For me.

Establishing Your Goals

If it is difficult to determine your goals, think about what brings you joy.

Example: Earn my bachelor's degree in forensic science by Jan. 2023.
Enroll, meet with my counselor, outline my course schedule

Example: Write my testimonial book by the Jan. 30th, 2023.
Steps Write one page per night

Here are steps you can take to create your goals:

- ❖ Pray and ask God to align your desires with His plans for your life.
- ❖ Brainstorm ideas (goals) you want to accomplish.
- ❖ Create steps you will take to accomplish your goals.
- ❖ Establish a timeline of when you want to accomplish your goals.
- ❖ Work towards accomplishing your goals.
- ❖ Check in to evaluate your progress.

Brainstorming

What are my goals? *(List each goal separately.)*

_____

_____

_____

_____

How important is each goal? *(Number them, with one being the most important.)*

_____

_____

_____

_____

What commitment am I going to make to accomplish these goals?

_____
_____
_____
_____
_____
_____

Who will be my accountability partner, and why? *(Someone to check in to ensure focus.)*

_____
_____
_____
_____
_____
_____

GOAL 1: _____

★ Time *(How much time do I have to put toward this goal?)*

```
┌─────────────────────────────────────────────────────┐
│                                                     │
│                                                     │
└─────────────────────────────────────────────────────┘
```

★ Effort *(What effort am I willing to put into accomplishing this goal?)*

```
┌─────────────────────────────────────────────────────┐
│                                                     │
│                                                     │
│                                                     │
└─────────────────────────────────────────────────────┘
```

★ Details *(How much attention will I give to this goal?)*

```
┌─────────────────────────────────────────────────────┐
│                                                     │
│                                                     │
│                                                     │
└─────────────────────────────────────────────────────┘
```

★ Action *(What steps will I take to accomplish this goal?)*

```
┌─────────────────────────────────────────────────────┐
│                                                     │
│                                                     │
│                                                     │
└─────────────────────────────────────────────────────┘
```

GOAL CHECK-IN

Document your progress in achieving your goal.

GOAL 2: _____

★ Time *(How much time do I have to put toward this goal?)*

```
┌─────────────────────────────────────────────────────┐
│                                                     │
│                                                     │
└─────────────────────────────────────────────────────┘
```

★ Effort *(What effort am I willing to put into accomplishing this goal?)*

```
┌─────────────────────────────────────────────────────┐
│                                                     │
│                                                     │
│                                                     │
└─────────────────────────────────────────────────────┘
```

★ Details *(How much attention will I give to this goal?)*

```
┌─────────────────────────────────────────────────────┐
│                                                     │
│                                                     │
│                                                     │
└─────────────────────────────────────────────────────┘
```

★ Action *(What steps will I take to accomplish this goal?)*

```
┌─────────────────────────────────────────────────────┐
│                                                     │
│                                                     │
│                                                     │
└─────────────────────────────────────────────────────┘
```

GOAL CHECK-IN

Document your progress in achieving your goal.

GOAL 3: _____

★ Time *(How much time do I have to put toward this goal?)*

>

★ Effort *(What effort am I willing to put into accomplishing this goal?)*

>

★ Details *(How much attention will I give to this goal?)*

>

★ Action *(What steps will I take to accomplish this goal?)*

>

GOAL CHECK-IN

Document your progress in achieving your goal.

GOAL 4: _____

★ Time *(How much time do I have to put toward this goal?)*

★ Effort *(What effort am I willing to put into accomplishing this goal?)*

★ Details *(How much attention will I give to this goal?)*

★ Action *(What steps will I take to accomplish this goal?)*

GOAL CHECK-IN

Document your progress in achieving your goal.

GOAL 5: _____

★ Time *(How much time do I have to put toward this goal?)*

★ Effort *(What effort am I willing to put into accomplishing this goal?)*

★ Details *(How much attention will I give to this goal?)*

★ Action *(What steps will I take to accomplish this goal?)*

GOAL CHECK-IN

Document your progress in achieving your goal.

I speak and pour positivity
into my life.

Daily Affirmations

Affirmations can help you overcome fear and build your self-confidence. It helps to have daily affirmations.

Some examples include:

- ❖ I am beautiful.
- ❖ I love my hair.
- ❖ I love my lips.
- ❖ I am enough.
- ❖ I can do this.
- ❖ I am going to conquer the day.
- ❖ I will walk confidently into the meeting.
- ❖ I will not be consumed by things I cannot control.

**WRITE YOUR AFFIRMATIONS
IN THE SPACE PROVIDED.**

Failure is not an option. That's why I keep pushing forward.

Journaling and Prayers

Nothing is Impossible. The word itself says, "I'm Possible!"
~Audrey Hepburn

STAY CONNECTED WITH FATIMA MCCOY-LEONARD, Ed.D.

Scan me!